The First Olympic Games

The country of Greece hosted the first Olympic Games in the valley of Olympia in 776 B.C. It was held to honor the Greek gods, especially king Zeus. The only event in the first 13 Olympic Games was a 200-meter footrace. Only male athletes were allowed to compete. As time passed, other events were added and females were allowed to compete as well. In 393 A.D., more than 1,000 years after the first Olympic Games, Emperor Theodosius ordered them stopped. The Olympic Games were not played again until 1896 when they became an international competition.

Choose a word from the story to fill in each blank. Draw a picture of the first Olympic Games in the space below.

first Olympic _____   king _____

country of _____   foot _____

valley of _____   international _____

The Olympic Symbol

The symbol for the Olympic Games is five interlocking rings that represent the continents of Africa, Asia, Australia, Europe, and North and South America. The colors of the rings are black, blue, green, red, and yellow. Every competing nation's flag has at least one of these colors.

Imagine you are an athlete from a new nation joining the Olympic Games. Design a flag for your new nation using the colors from the Olympic symbol.

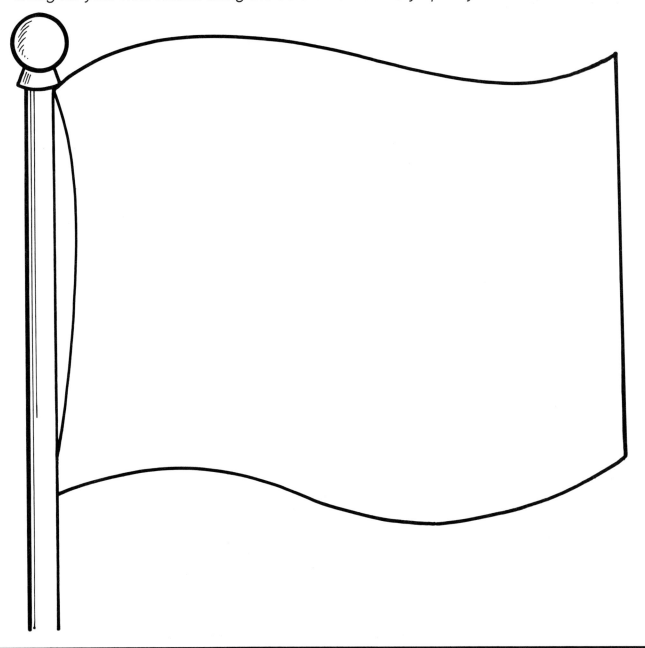

The Opening Ceremony

The Opening Ceremony of the Olympic Games is an amazing event. Athletes from around the world march into the stadium, the start of the Olympic Games is announced, the Olympic flag is raised, and hundreds of doves are released into the air as a symbol of peace.

Think of three ways to keep peace and friendship around the world. Write each idea on a dove.

The Olympic Oath

Part of the Opening Ceremony is the reading of the Olympic oath. The Olympic oath is a promise to compete fairly, follow the rules, and show good sportsmanship.

Write an oath for behavior on the playground. Include behaviors such as following rules and showing good sportsmanship.

OLYMPIC OATH

_____

_____

_____

_____

_____

_____

Lighting the Olympic Flame

The most exciting part of the Opening Ceremony is the lighting of the Olympic flame. Thousands of runners from around the world help carry a lit torch from Greece to the location of the Olympic Games. At the Opening Ceremony, the torch is used to light a large flame that will burn during the entire Olympic competition.

Help the runner find the way to the Opening Ceremony to light the Olympic flame.

Hosting the Olympic Games

The Olympic Games have been played in many countries throughout the world, including France, Australia, Canada, Spain, Germany, Italy, and the United States. It is a great honor to have the Olympic Games in your country.

Create an Olympic poster to convince the Olympic committee that your country is the best location for the Olympic Games.

 OLYMPIC POSTER

Olympic Medals

Men and women compete in the Olympic Games to show their excellence in sports. The top three athletes in each Olympic event receive a medal—a bronze medal for 3rd place, a silver medal for 2nd place, and a gold medal for winning the competition.

The medals look different at every Olympic Games. You have been chosen to design an Olympic gold medal. Draw what you think the next gold medal should look like.

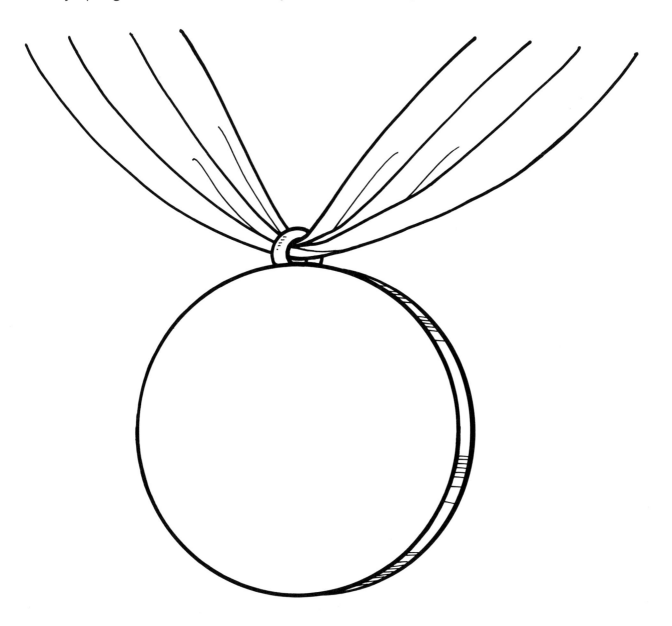

Olympic Events

Thousands of male and female athletes from over 190 nations compete in the Olympic Games. The Olympic Games consist of the Summer and Winter Games and include more than 30 sporting events. Special symbols are used to represent different Olympic events so they can be "read" by everyone no matter what language they speak.

Cut apart the names and symbols of the Olympic events. Complete the following activities with a partner.

1. Play the Olympic Memory Game. Turn all name and symbol cards face down. Take turns turning over one name card and one symbol card. If the name matches the symbol, keep them; if not, turn them face down again. The player with the most matches at the end of the game wins.

2. Match each symbol with its correct name and glue onto index cards. Separate the cards into two groups—Summer Games and Winter Games. Write *summer* or *winter* on the back of each card. Compare your answers with your classmates.

3. Create your own symbol cards. Draw a symbol for a game or event on an index card. Write its name on the back of the card. See if your partner can guess the game or event by looking at your symbol.

Olympic Events

Alpine skiing	Cycling	Diving
Soccer	Swimming	Ice hockey
Volleyball	Rowing	Wrestling

Olympic Events

Judo	Gymnastics	Speed skating
Equestrian (Horseback)	Figure skating	Track and field
Basketball	Boxing	Baseball

Creating an Olympic Event

A sport must be popular in at least 50 countries on three continents before it can become part of the Summer Games. A sport must be popular in at least 25 countries on two continents to be included in the Winter Games. There are more that 23 official summer sports and more than 7 official winter sports.

Create a unique sporting event for the Olympic Games. Draw a picture and write about your new Olympic event.

Becoming an Olympic Athlete

Athletes practice and train for many years to compete in the Olympic Games. Olympic athletes need to be dedicated, hard-working, and talented to make their Olympic dreams come true.

Write an Olympic champion "recipe." Under ingredients, list qualities and skills needed to become a top Olympic athlete. Then describe how the "ingredients" are used in Olympic competition.

How to Make an Olympic Champion

Ingredients:

_____   _____

_____   _____

_____   _____

Directions:

_____

_____

_____

_____

_____

Young Olympic Competitors

Sonja Henie of Norway was one of the youngest athletes to participate in the Olympic Games. She was only 10 years old when she figure skated her way into Olympic competition. Marjorie Gestring of the United States won a gold medal for diving at age 13. The youngest athlete to win an Olympic competition was a young French boy who won a gold medal for rowing in 1900. He was only 7 years old!

Imagine that you are the youngest competitor at the Olympic Games. Choose an event and write what happens to you when you compete against the older athletes.

Famous Olympic Athletes

Many great athletes have competed in the Olympic Games. In 1936, Jesse Owens of the United States won four gold medals in track and field. Mark Spitz, a United States swimmer, set an Olympic record in 1972 by winning seven gold medals. In 1988, swimmer Kristin Otto of East Germany became the first woman to win six gold medals in the Olympic Games.

Make an Olympic quilt of famous athletes from an Olympic event. Draw a picture of the event in the center. Use pictures and words to show an Olympic medal winner in each corner.

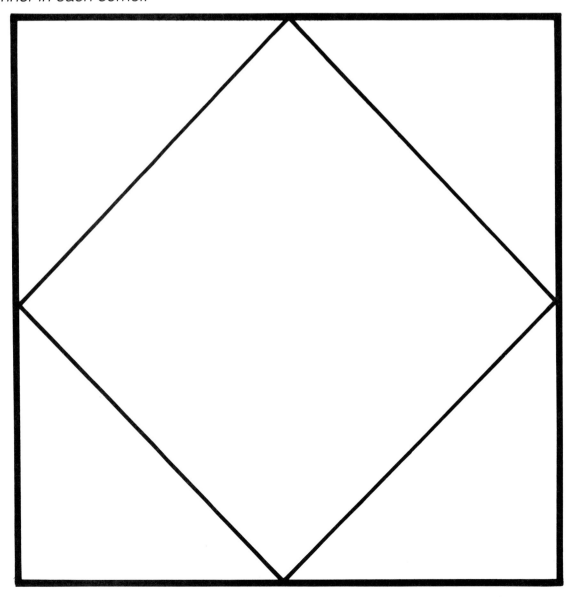

Special Athletes

Some athletes overcome special challenges to become champions. Wilma Rudolph suffered through polio, double pneumonia, and scarlet fever when she was a child. She could not use her left leg for several years, but she was determined to become a star athlete. Wilma Rudolph reached her goal in 1960 when she won three Olympic gold medals in track and field.

Write about a goal that you worked hard to reach. Fill in the newspaper article announcing your success.

Olympic Press Paper   XII www www

READ ALL ABOUT IT!

_____

_____

_____

_____

_____

_____

The Closing Ceremony

In the Closing Ceremony, athletes enter the stadium for the last time and say good-bye to all their new friends. The country where the next Olympic Games will be held raises their flag and invites everyone to the future competition. The Olympic Games are officially over and the Olympic flame is put out. The athletes return home with the rewards and memories of competing in the Olympic Games.

Think of the Olympic Games from start to finish. Look at the Olympic stadium. Match each picture with the correct description by writing a letter on each blank line.

A. Awarding medals to Olympic athletes

B. Reading the Olympic oath

C. Releasing doves for world peace

D. Athletes marching around the stadium

E. The Olympic symbol

F. Runners competing in track and field

G. Lighting the Olympic flame

(Answers: 1. C, 2. E, 3. G, 4. F, 5. B, 6. A, 7. D)